AF633315

From

Western Science

To

Liberation Technology

From Western Science *To* Liberation Technology

Winin Pereira

Earthcare Books

From Western Science to Liberation Technology, 2018
EARTHCARE BOOKS
10 Middleton Street, Kolkata 700071, India

Phone : 033 22296551 / 22276190 / 022 23542420
Email : earthcarebooks@gmail.com
Website : www.earthcarebooks.com

First published by EARTHCARE BOOKS in 1993
Fifth impression: 2018

© Earthcare Books

ISBN 81-85861-20-x

Computerset : Compuset International, Kolkata
Cover Design: Deepa Balsavar

Printed by : Unique Phototype, Kolkata

CONTENTS

Acknowledgements

My grateful thanks are due to the Adivasis who introduced me to liberation technology, in particular Janiya Ghatal and Gopal Rade, and to Vasudha Ambiye. Thanks also to Jeremy Seabrook, Manek Mistry, Raajan Singh, Celine D'Souza, Jeeten Bhat, Suresh Devasahayam, Subhash Sule, Ravi and Nikhil Pereira for their invaluable contributions to this work.

Winin Pereira
1993

Introduction

Western science and technology* are usually seen as necessary and sufficient to provide solutions for most of the problems of inequitable development today. But can they lead to a "self-reliant and non-exploitative social order"?

From its inception, Western science brought forth technology designed for the domination of a large proportion of humanity through war and colonial exploitation. Economic exploitation provided the funds that fueled further science and technology, which fed more exploitation, in a positive feedback system. Cultural domination ensured that Western science's claim to be the sole valid set of knowledge was not challenged. Western science is symbiotic with Western society: neither can exist in

---

* The terms "Western science" and "Western technology", as used here, apply to what has been developed in the West as well as in other countries which have emulated or are trying to copy the Western method. The term "Western scientist", however, does not apply to those, in the West or here, who are already aware of these problems of Western science and are trying to correct them.

the state it is in without the other.

Domination requires an exploitable set, which in this case has been the Two-Thirds World and Nature. If we attempt to detach Western science and technology and to graft it on to a less exploitative society, we could be coerced and constrained to grow unjustly and produce equally bad fruit. We will either exploit the peoples of other nations weaker than us or the weaker sections of our own population, as is happening to a large extent already.

For those who are concerned with justice, it appears that the Westernised system cannot be relevant to India, nor to the West itself.

Traditional systems of science and technology, which sustained civilisations for centuries till Western conquerors tried to forcibly destroy them, appear to be possible alternatives for a more liberating system.

1

Western Science & Technology

WESTERN SCIENCE & DOMINATION

Science is seen, by some Western scientists them selves, as giving the power to exploit. Kurt Mendelssohn, FRS, an Oxford professor, in his book "Science & Western Domination", asserts that science is "the key to world dominion". "The burden of this book", he claims, "has been to show that the consistent development of natural philosophy has given to the white race the power of domination over others"[2]

Western S & T's Contribution to War

Western science and technology are essential generators of power for political and industrial structures.

Mendelssohn writes: "The first landmark, and probably the most important in the history of white domination, was reached in 1313 when Berthold Schwarz . . . fired the first cannon ball . . . The Chinese knew how to make gunpowder long before but, being peaceful by nature, used it exclusively for fireworks".[3] The technology for making gunpowder travelled west during the Middle Ages. Muskets and cannons, developed during the 14th century, exploited its power as a propellant.[4]

Galileo used his knowledge of falling objects to calculate projectile trajectories and determine the elevation of guns required to hit their human targets more accurately.[5] Descartes' "analytical geometry not only lent itself to the elucidation of planetary orbits, but even more so to ballistics, which had now become an exact science".[6]

Mendelssohn adds: "Firearms certainly played an important part in the white subjugation of the rest of the world. Sometimes, as in one of the first trials of the machine-gun, a handful of Europeans could completely rout an army of thousands of tribesmen (sic)".[7] This superiority in human extermination technology helped convince the Europeans that they were superior to the "natives" in all other respects, too.

"From Thales to Nobel, via Archimedes and Leonardo, (Western scientists') objectives have been clear. Find something that will make a big bang, work out how to send it where it will do most damage . . . ".[8] To which list must be added Fermi, Oppenheimer, Sakharov and the army of "defence scientists" who have worked for war and are working for war now.

Fritz Haber is well known for his contribution to the synthesis of ammonia from atmospheric nitrogen. During the 1914-18 European war, Germany would have quickly collapsed after its imports of saltpetre from Chile were cut off had not the Haber-Bosch process provided alternative nitrates for explosives. Haber also recommended the use of chemical gas warfare and worked vigorously to make it successful.[9]

The decision to drop nuclear bombs on Hiroshima and Nagasaki was taken in secret by a small number of military personnel, politicians and scientists, who controlled the technology. Oppenheimer admitted that "The twin evils of secrecy and control strike at the very nature of what science is and what it is for".[10] Western science and technology created and sustained the "super" powers. Kissinger hailed the scientific revolution for having removed "all technical limits to the exercise of power".[11] Nuclear bombs, after all, give the possessor absolute power, the power to destroy all life on earth. And with absolute nuclear power goes absolute corruption.

The universities and other academic institutions have contributed to military technology for centuries. The Massachusetts Institute of Technology Instrumentation Laboratory played an essential role in the development of missile guidance systems in the US. The unit became the Charles Stark Draper Laboratory, named after its founder, an MIT professor of aeronautics and astronautics, who died in 1987.[12]

Today, most universities in the US support themselves by undertaking projects for the "defence" department. Their scholars have helped develop, among other things, high-tech fuel-air explosives (FAEs) which the US armed forces used with gruesome effects on human targets in Iraq. With weapons like FAEs, former Defence Secretary Robert S McNamara boasted, the US could "do with conventional weapons what previously had required nuclear munitions", the latter being the US' standard by which weapons are to be judged. FAEs disperse a cloud of highly volatile fuel which is detonated to produce a massive explosion, sucking up oxygen and creating firestorm-like conditions. Human beings caught in the target area thus suffer first the shock of the concussion, then suffocation, and finally incineration. University-based research focused on "improving" the weapons with computer simulations.[13]

These scientists claim that Western science is neutral and so they bear no responsibility for the consequences of their actions. When questioned, they denied having anything to do with weapons development, insisting that there was no connection between scientific means and military ends. Some professors working on FAEs compared them to the discovery of fire, which can be used either to cook food or incinerate human beings.[14]

War's Contribution to Western S & T

Electronic computers were first developed to break enemy codes in the second World War. Hitler's—or rather, Wernher von Braun's—V-2 rockets which killed thousands of civilians in the 1939-45 war, formed the basis of the American space programme. Intercontinental ballistic missiles, all descended from the V-2 and designed to kill millions, now send out planetary probes and astronomical telescopes. Spy satellites gave birth to satellite communications, Star TV, and remote sensing.

Some areas of apparently "pure" science, especially the study of the Earth's gravitational Field, owe a lot to the search for greater missile accuracy. The Human Genome project is being promoted largely for military purposes, the detailed knowledge of human gene sequences having a special importance in the selective targeting of biological weapons.[15]

One professor claimed that "doing weapons research was a sure way of staying at the forefront of technology". The fact is that the major incentive for all significant developments in technology has been warfare. What would be the state of Western science and technology today if all scientists had refused, or refuse now, to promote military science?

Western S & T's Contributions to Exploitation

However, a larger proportion of Western science's output worked, and now works, not with bangs but with scarcely a whisper. It is claimed that the expeditions of Magellan and others were voyages of exploration to understand the planet. In a sense this was correct, for to those explorers, the peoples they "discovered" were mere objects of "scientific" study. Like crops and minerals, they were passively waiting to be utilised. Their existence had no value, till they were "discovered" by the Europeans, which "discoveries" conferred (exploitable) worth. The "natives"—human beings as well as plants and animals—were seen to be as expendable as material resources, just as the surviving "tribals"—Native Americans, aborigines in Australia—are treated today.

The continuing "celebrations" of centenaries of those "discoveries" shows that such attitudes are still alive and widely accepted. For us, who were on the receiving end of such weapons and voyages, and who felt no need to be "discovered", the opinion of Western science should be different. However, cultural domination ensures that we continue to be enslaved, with our mental territories occupied by the West.[16] So we applaud such voyages of "discovery" even though they were or are intended to harm us.

Alfred Russel Wallace, a contemporary of Darwin, who also proposed an evolutionary theory, saw natural selection as working on races and nations, and complacently accepted the "inevitable extinction of all those low and mentally undeveloped populations with which Europeans come in contact. The Red Indian in North America, and in Brazil, the Tasmanian, Australian and New Zealander . . . [17] The destruction of indigenous tribal groups still takes place in a large number of countries, including ours, in the name of "progress" based on the Western model of development.

Early anthropological science, from cranial anthropology to social Darwinism, served the sole purpose of elevating the white male to the level of superior beings and delegating the other "races"—and all women—to subhuman levels. Such theories were not just fads but were considered exact sciences in their heyday, backed up with reams of statistical data, selectively collected or wrongly interpreted, and combined with a distortion of Darwin's theory of evolution to justify a priori prejudices. Such "science" is current even now. Such theories scientifically sanctioned and even sanctified the subjugation and genocide of conquered Native peoples and slaves.

During 200 years of occupation of India, the British used science to further their commercial and political interests. A botanical garden was set up in 1787 near Calcutta to grow teak for ship-building. An observatory was established in 1790 at Madras to survey the treacherous Coromandel coast. A trigonometrical survey of India was started in 1800 when the conquest of Tipu Sultan gave the British the peninsular of India. The Geological Survey was set up in 1854 when coal was needed for steam navigation.[19]

The technology that Western science spawned made widespread colonial conquests possible. Steamships enabled the voyages from Europe to the occupied territories to be considerably shortened. In America, the transcontinental railways hastened the decimation of the Native population. The railway system is commonly assumed to be one of the benefits bestowed on India by the British, but its rapid expansion took place after our first war of independence in 1857, when the British discovered the need to move their troops around quickly. The railways played a major role in the economic rape of our traditional agricultural and industrial system. They still serve as arteries which enable the cities to bleed the countryside into poverty and unsustainability.

Mendelssohn writes: "The silent giant of electrodynamics has provided the white man (sic) with a sledge-hammer tool to assert his dominance over the globe. However, he also has a little sister (sic) called electronics who is less obtrusive and less powerful, but whose gentle grip on the globe has held the rest of mankind (sic) in even tighter bondage."[20] That was in 1976; electronics has now grown very big indeed and, via computers and communication satellites, is the main mode of cultural dominance.

Technological domination also enabled the West to ravage the global resource base. Environmental colonialism now enables bulldozers and chainsaws to annihilate tropical forests in order to provide hamburgers for the US and hardwoods for Japan. The West claims the right to displace—or drown—millions in the Maldives, Bangladesh and other low-lying countries, through global warming, caused mainly by the emission of greenhouse gases in the West.

While some may agree that Western science has been and is now supported by unjust means, they may still hope that its basic methods or theories could be used to build up a new, just science. But Western science and technology are the tools that unjust societal structures have developed to support themselves. It is doubtful whether tools designed for injustice can also be used to serve just ends. It should be obvious that any science driven by the same motives, funded by the same sources, and with the same structure, cannot solve the problems which Western science has created.

Exploitation's Contribution to Western S & T

Western science has, reciprocally, benefited enormously from colonisation.

Western scientists were urged to understand and explore Nature by those who wished to increase their economic and political power. "Isaac Newton may have thought he was interested in the mechanisms that controlled the movement of planets. But his thoughts were triggered (so some modern historians of science would have us believe) by the need of the time to expand world trade, and therefore to improve navigation at sea. That thought, at least, 'was what inspired the Establishment that supported his researches, and which finally made him a member of Parliament, president of the Royal Society, and master of the Mint."[21] Without such financial support, it is doubtful whether he would have had the leisure to watch falling apples.

The occupied territories—first the Americas with their gold and silver, and later India with its vast range of agricultural and industrial products—financed much of British scientific research, freeing it from its dependence on wealthy but often unreliable patrons.[22] It was such extensive financing that allowed Western science and technology to grow as it did.

In the 1780s, the Abbe Reynal, speaking of the "discovery" of America, claimed that "This great event hath improved the construction of ships, navigation, geography, astronomy, medicine, natural history, and some other branches of knowledge; and these advantages have not been attended with any known inconvenience". It was attended with more than inconvenience as Far as the Natives were concerned. Reynal admits that the domains of the Indies "have given splendour, power, and wealth, to the states which founded them. . . . Europe is indebted to the New World for a few conveniences, and a few luxuries . . . so cruelly obtained. . . ."[23]

Industry's benefits from War and Exploitation

Large corporations with Financial stakes in weapons R & D are central to what President Eisenhower first called the "military-industrial complex".

But even the "civilian" fallout of killing technology has its problems. After the 1914-18 European War, the manufacturers of nitrates used in explosives, promoted their use as synthetic fertilisers. Chemicals developed for nerve gas weapons led to synthetic insecticides. Turning swords into ploughshares for economic reasons, does not necessarily lead to good agriculture. The list of such "fallout" is endless, and much of it has turned out to be as harmful as the radioactive variety, since it was and is used for economic warfare.

Such symbiotic and harmonious development of academic science, the military establishment and industry has now come full circle. The West is winding up its chemical warfare laboratories, giving the impression that it is so concerned about their dangers that it would rather not take the risk of even stocking old weapons. However, this sudden piety hides the fact that they no longer need them. The pesticides industry with its wide range of herbicides, including the deadly 2,4-D used in Vietnam, can produce as much damage in the "enemy's" countries as any plain poison. Wiping out harvests in whole regions is easily possible by spraying commercial herbicides from the air, an added advantage being that no one can trace its origin.

The case of the indigo dye is an example of the process of exploitation, typifying the Western scientific-industrial system. For centuries, indigo was obtained in India from several plants, usually growing wild and used extensively in the Indian textile industry. In the 18th century, access to natural dyes was crucial to the growing European textile industry. The British appropriated the indigo technology, since they saw in indigo an item for monopoly trade and a vast market ripe for "development". They forced Indian farmers to cultivate it even when it was unprofitable for them to do so.

By the 1850s, British chemists were trying to find synthetic substitutes for indigo, and so were their German colleagues. Much research was carried out by scientists working for Badische Anilin and Soda-Fabric AG (BASF), Hoechst AG and Bayer AG. By 1897, BASF was mass-producing synthetic indigo. By 1901, the quality and price of BASF's and Hoechst's synthetic dye reduced German demand for the Indian product by around 40%.

Synthetic indigo, among other dyes, proved so profitable that the major German dyestuffs manufactures, brought close together during the 1914-18 War, formalised their marriage of cartelisation as I G Farben Industrie in 1926.[24]

During the 1939-45 European war, IG Farben built and operated a massive chemical plant at Auschwitz with slave labour. About 300,000 concentration-camp workers passed through the plant at Auschwitz, of which at least 25,000 were worked to death.[25] Others died in I G Farben's drug testing programme.

Letters of the company to the camp at Auschwitz reveal what such corporate power leads to: "In contemplation of experiments with a new soporific drug, we would appreciate your procuring for us a number of women. . . . We received your answer but consider the price of 200 marks a woman excessive.

We propose to pay not more than 170 marks a head. If agreeable, we will take possession of the women. We need approximately 150. . . . Received the order of 150 women. Despite their emaciated condition, they were found satisfactory. We shall keep you posted on developments concerning this experiment. . . . The tests were made. All subjects died. We shall contact you shortly on the subjects of a new load"[26]

Twelve top I G Farben executives were sentenced to various terms of imprisonment for slavery and mistreatment offences at the Nuremberg war crime trials. The Allies broke up I G Farben into effectively three companies, Hoechst, BASF and Bayer, insisting that none of the convicted war criminals be appointed to the boards of these companies. Once Allied control loosened, Hoechst in June 1955 appointed Friedrich Jaehne, one of the twelve sentenced, to its supervisory board; by September of that year he was elected Chairman. Bayer appointed Fitz ter Meer, sentenced to 7 years at Nuremberg, as Chairman of its board in 1956".[27]

Hoechst and Bayer—both of which depended on indigo for their early growth—had the fourth and fifth largest sales of pharmaceuticals in the world in 1991, respectively. Their present behaviour reflects their war-time morals: Many of the drugs sold by Hoechst in the Two-Thirds World are not sold in Germany, are not essential, are hazardous or cause harm, perhaps even death, to their users.[28]

Cultural Domination

As a reward for their contribution to politicians and

the military, Western scientists are granted privileges of affluence, status secrecy, working funds and a symbolic share of power. It is only a small, arrogant step to perceive in that power a providential, privileged access to "truth" which is promoted as an absolute system. For Western science monopolises knowledge and intellectually colonises people.

Habermas says: "Scientism' means science's belief in itself: that is, the conviction that we can no longer understand science as one form of possible knowledge, but rather must identify knowledge with science".[29]

Western science itself cannot prove its claim to a monopoly on knowledge of reality: such proof can only come from outside Western science. The evidence is that, even if its theories of the material universe are valid, Western science ignores a large part of reality. It is an incomplete system of knowledge, if not a false one.

The imposition of a single "science" necessarily means the destruction of innumerable locally created "sciences"—systems of knowledge. This mental marginalisation, the counterpart of colonial material conquest, is a more subtle—but much more devastating—from of domination. We help the process to continue and expand by consenting to being exploited, by being dependent on and promoting Western science and technology.

It is irrational to expect that Western science can be used for liberation from the very exploitation that it continuously creates. The promotion of Western science here can, at most, empower us to dominate others.

Western science required and requires large funds for carrying out its investigations. Such supporting funds could only be accumulated through unjust processes.

Western scientists had patrons in the old days—royalty and other members of the "nobility". The latter accumulated their wealth from internal exploitation of the peasantry and working classes and, later, from the slave trade and colonial extraction.

Galileo's works are glaringly obsequious to the princes, dukes, and others who financed him.[30] Tycho Brahe, the astronomer, belonged to a Danish "noble" family. In 1576 King Frederick III gave Brahe the island of Ven and a grant that provided him with a large income. On that island Brahe built Uraniborg, his research institute, in which he developed the instruments required for accurate observation. But when Frederick died, Brahe's research funds dwindled, compelling him to move to Prague where Emperor Rudolph of Bohemia funded further research.[31]

Priestley first isolated oxygen in 1774 in a laboratory set up in the home of William Fitzmaurice, Earl of Shelbourne, who financed him.[32] The Royal Institution of Great Britain was founded in 1799 by Count Rumford, described as a traitor, spy, opportunist, womaniser, inventor, plagiarist and expert on heat.[33]

The development of the British textile industry, which ushered in the industrial revolution, was financed by capital extracted from the Americas and India. The machine-made products brought immense fortunes by the transfer of wealth through the forced sale of manufactured goods, which disemployed hand spinners and weavers in India. The need for improved steam engines to drive the machinery led to the development of thermodynamics. The need for dyes to replace those imported from the tropics contributed much to progress in organic chemistry. Each "advance" in science, in turn, resulted in "progress" in technological and economic exploitation which resulted in the further accumulation of surplus funds.

Today, Western science is wholly supported by the profits of those who, scientists sometimes claim, "abuse" Western science for the profitable exploitation of others. No doubt, other professionals are equally predatory or parasitic in that unjust system, but that does not absolve Western scientists, who often claim to be above such sordid matters.

While early scientists may be excused for being unable to predict that their work would be sued for destructive and antisocial purposes instead of being an unmixed blessing for humankind, there is little justification today—other than that of the pervasiveness of the unjust system—for the extensive, practically universal "misuse" of Western science and its products.

It is not only work on or near the leading edge of science that requires money. All scientists who conduct formal research, whether pure or applied, require salaries and funds for laboratories and the expensive equipment on which they are totally dependent. Their ability to carry on such research results from the production of poverty elsewhere in the global system. Some complain that the money used for space extravaganzas could have been better used for relieving world hunger. But those extravaganzas were made feasible only by the prior production of such hunger. Billions can be spent on space research only if billions are first impoverished, mostly in the Two-Thirds World.

Much of Western science and technology is supported by big business. Glaxo needs to make more than a billion pounds profit a year to support its research and development. Every person who is seduced into buying a tin of Glaxo's Farex, a tube of Colgate's toothpaste, a cake of Hindusthan Lever's soap, a strip of Hoechst's Analgin or a Union Carbide dry cell, contributes her/his mite to Western industrial as well as fundamental research: to research in particle physics, biotechnology, superconductivity, fifth-generation computers, and everything else. The purchase of "high" technology products by us from the West contributes much more.

Most of the science research in Western universities is being funded by industries, the "defence" establishment, or by their governments who in turn obtain their funds from industry. Today it is economic interest which mainly drives science in the direction in which industry wants it to go. With government funding being drastically reduced in most of the West, academics are compelled to go to industry, begging bowl in hand, for funds. Research projects are then naturally tailored and shaped to fit the needs of industry rather than the goals of an independent science. Industrial representatives, overt or covert, are often on the committees that determine how government funds are spent.[34]

Sales by companies reliant on physics rose from

£40 billion in 1980 to £86 billion in 1989.[35] The nuclear industry is one which cannot operate without physics. Others included were telecommunications, car manufacturing and aerospace and the machine tool industry, which supports many other engineering and manufacturing operations.[36] All these determine the direction in which physics itself is moving.

The positive feedback of exploitation fostering Western science, science fostering exploitation, is the process which enabled and still enables Western science as well as the Western industrial system to "progress" so rapidly. It is this symbiosis—the dependent connection between the two of more "organisms"—which enables them to achieve what neither would accomplish alone. It is this symbiosis which makes Western science inseparable from exploitation.

The annual expenditure per researcher in Britain in 1990 was £73,000 and in Germany £128,000.[37] If we in India can afford such funds to work on Western science, then those funds must come from the exploitation of our own citizens or other "less developed" nations. There is no way in which a non-exploiter can accumulate such large amounts. We, who are ourselves being exploited by such a science, should be more sensitive about using it to exploit others.

The latest trend towards privatisation of all research must limit studies only to those which can be commercialised, with further possibilities of dominance and exploitation. A December 1991 report of the British Parliamentary Office of Science and Technology claimed that a pound spent on supercomputers could be a thousand times more beneficial than a pound given to pensioners. In practice, this would require depriving pensioners of their annual £10 bonus and use of the £100 million it saves to buy supercomputers[38]—starving pensioners to buy computers. It is now openly being suggested that scientific academic institutions start paying British members of parliament—just as other industrial lobbyists do—so that they may use their influence to get more funds.[39]

Western science has fallen from fawning on patrons to begging industry to bribing politicians because of its dependency on large funding.

Western Science as a Common Heritage

It is often asserted that humankind has an inherent need to understand the universe, to find meaning in it. It is claimed that the "truth" that Western science uncovers about reality is available to all, and hence, "science is the common heritage of mankind (sic)". Any "abuses" of Western science from which people may suffer, should be considered "payment" for this service.

Although the word "heritage" is neutral—what is inherited can be good or bad for the heir—it is implied that the inheritors have free access to Western science and/or obtain some advantage from it. If Western science and technology themselves are a common heritage, then everyone so inclined should be in a position to practice them. Equal access should mean equal capability to repeat or carry out research in the directions in which it is going. But mere costs make Western scientific research and technological innovation inaccessible to most people and most nations. Many institutions cannot afford to subscribe to all the scientific journals being published today. The cost of just one "instrument", the Superconducting Supercollider (SSC), was estimated at more than $8 billion, its chief purpose being to "discover" one particle, the Higgs boson. The usual argument is that fundamental physics will help all people in the long run, but fundamental physics' discoveries almost always first helped to exploit others. Further, Western scientific knowledge itself is being privatised. An increasing number of Western scientists, working for business and "defence" establishments, are under contract not to publish or even talk about their work.

A majority of the people are not even aware of Western science's theories, while awareness alone does not mean understanding. Can people get pleasure from a science they are not aware of or do not understand? Few get mental satisfaction from theories that space is curved or that quarks come with queer flavours. Few scientists themselves can understand such theories, but these may not be capable of adding to or even criticising them. "Only a few people can keep up with the rapidly advancing frontier of knowledge", says Stephen Hawking, "and they have to devote their whole time to it and specialise in a small area. The rest of the population has little idea of the advances that are being made..."[40]

Moreover, scientists themselves have doubts about whether they are discovering "reality" or merely mathematising fantasies. " . . . Abdus Salam is hopeful of recent work with 26 dimensions, which can be made equivalent to 26 fundamental fields in a two—dimensional spacetime. The 'incandescent beauty of this theory' manifests itself in the uniqueness of certain (untestable?) predictions. . . . ' One can only hope nature is aware of our work on all this,' Salam says wistfully."[41]

The claim that all people benefit from Western technology is equally questionable. Take the case of the planetary probes. Perhaps a hundred scientists are directly interested in Neptune and a few thousand may have actually been involved in the construction, launching and monitoring of the probe, though they may not have been interested in Neptune itself. There will be some indirect "benefits" to the military and industrial establishments. The general US population gets a vicarious pleasure in their nation having done the job. And the rest of the world may get a similar secondhand pleasure in what their humankind has accomplished. The majority who lack bread have been conditioned to applaud such circuses—as the Roman population was. The suffering masses who fight poverty are the modern gladiators. And just as the Roman gladiators had to salute Caesar before they were killed, those "who are about to die" of hunger are trained to salute the scientists. Such pleasure from pain is similar to that which we Indians had been schooled to get from the existence of the "great and glorious" British Empire.

Nothing seems more useful and benign to humankind in general than weather satellites which are touted as being able to predict, not only normal rainfall, but also cyclones and hurricanes thus eliminating much destruction and loss of life. But things do not work out that way. The terrible cyclones which devastated Bangladesh were predicted well in advance but it did not help the people in its path. If a small part of the billions that had been spent on the satellite system had been used instead to build storm shelters on high ground and more embankments to protect low laying areas, it would have been far more effective in saving lives.

High technology mega-projects like big dams and power stations further impoverish the pauperised who contribute much to government revenue through indirect taxes.

Science itself contributed enormously to the robbery of what has been claimed to be the common heritage of the peoples of the conquered territories. The Royal Botanical Gardens at Kew, founded in the second half of the 18th century, sent collectors all over the world to find and gather plant specimens. They sent back not just plants and seeds but articles made from plant materials—baskets and bowls, cloths and dyestuffs, medicinal drugs and resins—as well as detailed descriptions of how to process them. This botanical imperialism not only provided Europe with plenty of raw materials and finished products, unobtainable by any other means, but also served well the needs of building and sustaining further empires. When planters in the West Indies requested a cheap source of food for their slaves, Captain Bligh and The Bounty was sent to Tahiti to collect young breadfruit trees for them.[42]

The term "common heritage" is itself being used as an excuse for much present-day robbery of the genetic resources of the Two-Thirds World. Western biotechnologists claim that the thousands of varieties of food crops carefully selected and cultivated, of plants tested and used for centuries for medicinal purposes, are the common heritage of mankind. This claim leaves them free to use the genes from them for genetic modification of commercialisable crops, with patents making the modifications so private that the original preservers of the gene will be unable to use it themselves.

The patent system itself was a fallout of Western science. Whereas earlier all inventors freely shared their innovations with their community, the commercialisation of science required the inventor to be "protected" from competition. It is quite common to hear that the publication of scientific papers has been help up to give lawyers time to file their patent applications.

There is a more unpleasant manner in which Western scientists use the heritage of the Two-Thirds World. Its populations are freely used as guinea-pigs—often with the full cooperation of local scientists—to test out malaria and leprosy vaccines, contraceptives and other drugs. Much AIDS research in Africa involves Western scientists, providing them with degrees and careers.[43]

Because Western S&T does not benefit a majority of people, it has become essential for that science to sell itself to non-scientists. Just like commercial advertisers, scientists loudly proclaim science and technology's benefits, hardly ever mentioning its exploitative costs, assuming that the "lay" public are gullible enough to appreciate their role as omniscient experts.

The demands of self-interest require that scientists deprecate those outside their establishments who question their authority. Such persons—environmentalists, antinuclear, antidam activists and many others—are called crazy, antinational, ignorant and uninformed, even while the scientists refuse to divulge the data on which they make their claims.

The promotion of nuclear energy as a "green" energy source shows that such scientists either are ignorant of the quantities of carbon dioxide and radioactive pollutants that are produced or that they are willing to suppress and distort information so that they may preserve their jobs.

Even the West's "low" technology products cannot reach more than a tiny proportion of humankind because of its use of polluting power sources and scarce resources. If all the peoples of the Earth were to miraculously reach the same level of consumption that the West has today, critical resource and pollution crises would occur within a few years.

The "appropriate technology" promoted by the West is also often engineered to exploit. All too frequently it is a method of selling their unsuitable, outdated technology through books, videos, journals, "expert" consultants and international conferences.

Western science could be, at most, a doubtful heritage of all affluent humankind.

WESTERN SCIENCE AS SELF-DESTRUCTIVE & UNSUSTAINABLE

Soon after Hiroshima was bombed, Bertrand Russell asked in the House of Lords: "Is it possible for a scientific society to continue to exist, or must such a society inevitably bring itself to destruction?"[44]

The power that Western science has bestowed has resulted in a spectacularly irrational situation. Politicians and militarists now claim that, in order to ensure a nation's survival, they must have, at an ever ready state of launch, the nuclear weapons to destroy all life on earth several times over. Scientists of smaller nations while asserting that megascience is essential for their nation's defence, may not have this extreme objective in mind, but they certainly aim at the efficient production of mass mortality.

In addition to the ultimate injustice of a possible nuclear holocaust, Western science has bequeathed another questionable heritage in the form of its "successes". It is often claimed that the success of Western science is proved by Western affluence and increasing consumption, highly productive Western industry and agriculture, space exploration, satellite communications, and so on However, all these give the appearance of stunning success for the system's parts even while each contributes to the exhaustion of the finite resources of the planet and to the damage—perhaps irreversible—of delicate environmental balances. Even without the "successes" of its nuclear, biological and chemical weapons, Western science's "gifts" of global climatic change and the weakened ozone layer, Chernobyl-type disasters, and about 100,000 untested chemicals dumped into the environment, can eliminate much, if not all, life on the planet. Each "success", like the "success" of a cancerous tumour, is contributing to the death of the system as a whole.

Those who contribute to the tumour rarely realise that the tumour is malignant. In fact, each participant in the tumour's system, with his/her bounded rationality, sees its rapid growth as triumphant. One reason why this malignancy is not easily visible is that every harmful consequence furnishes an opportunity for "advanced" technology to "cure" the damage produced by the old technology. While technology is thus made to appear benign and essential, the harm has to appear before it can be "cured" and much damage is always left uncorrected. Further, Western science's symbiosis with industry conditions it to see that the harm produced is an economic "benefit" because it adds to the Gross National Product: detoxifying the environment is applauded as a multi-billion-dollar business opportunity.

There is built-in-self-destruction in much of Western science. Genes from landraces are required in order to breed new crop varieties that can withstand the pests created by synthetic pesticides. But the wide deployment of such new varieties is destroying the very sources which are essential for producing new crops. The technology, claimed to produce more food, thus ensures its own elimination which must result in a drastic decrease in future food production.

Technology should be judged, not by whether it can take us to the moon or Mars, but by whether it will help us survive on earth. All the comforts and conveniences that Western science has produced, from electricity to easy transport, put together, cannot balance our extinction in the other pan. The production of each "benefit" inevitably adds to the extinction pan, since a "high standard of living" embodies a high standard of pollution and resource consumption, a high level of violence to the earth. It is, literally, costing the earth.

Most Western scientists believe that there is no limit to their ability to cope with their science's own deficiencies. They insist that all the problems science has created will be solved as it learns more; that more technological interventions will fix the problems caused by their earlier ones. The agricultural effects of global climatic change will be taken care of by the biotechnology revolution; new species of plants and animals will be invented, even while Western technology eliminates or endangers thousands of natural species every year. The production of greenhouse gases will be reduced by the use of nuclear energy, though that will produce more Chernobyl events. The ozone holes will be patched up by generating high-powered radio beams which will ionize the chlorine in the layer and so make it less effective in destroying ozone, though the generation of those beams will add their own pollution. New chemicals will be less polluting, though Western science has no way of guaranteeing that any chemical is completely safe.

The use of technological fixes is a process in which each problem is "solved" by producing multiple sub-problems, leading to an explosive chain reaction. The belief that this can provide sustainable development is superstition. Positive feedback processes need a self-limiting mechanism or they become unstable and destroy themselves. As of now, none seems to be operative.

Although Stephen Hawking states that "The eventual goal of science is to provide a single theory that describes the whole universe", he admits that "it turns out to be very difficult to describe the universe all in one go". So, science "breaks the problem up into bits", invents "a number of partial theories", each of which "predicts a certain limited class of observations, neglecting the effects of other quantities . . . It may be that this approach is completely wrong".[45] Moreover, Hawking concedes that though in the past "scientific discovery has conveyed a survival advantage", it "is not so clear that this is still the case; our scientific discoveries may well destroy us all . . . "[46]

The "survival advantage" that Hawking claims for past discoveries has been put to question with the environmental crises which have arisen because of Western science's incomplete knowledge, plain ignorance and premature interventions in Nature made on this basis.

Western science and its symbiotic economic and industrial systems are merely small sub-systems within the whole system of the planet and the universe. One can have a closed sub-system which is internally rational and valid, but such reduced rationality may be invalidated when it interacts with other systems in which it is embedded.

There are several reasons for Western science's ignorance. In some cases the data is insufficient, and there may not even be awareness of what needs to be collected. The ignorance could also be due to the absence of full theoretical understanding. The formula for the conversion of mass into energy is deceptively simple, but there were no accompanying theories which could predict the problems caused by radioactive fallout and waste storage. Western science could not foresee that spraying DDT would weaken birds' eggshells. CFCs were claimed to be ideal chemicals because they were stable—under laboratory conditions. Even when satellite instruments showed that the ozone layer was being depleted over the Antarctic, the data were dismissed as instrumental errors for years, because no such phenomenon had been anticipated. The hole was noticed only when a land-based sensor showed the ozone anomaly.[47]

There are numerous examples of the interactions of Western science, hailed as outstanding "progress" when they were discovered, which its later "advances" revealed to be harmful. There are the unsustainable consequences of using high-yielding varieties of crops, and synthetic fertilisers and pesticides. There are the large number of pharmaceutical drugs, initially hailed as modern miracles, but later withdrawn because of their "side-effects". It is not particular practices that are being questioned now, but the whole agricultural, health and other "sciences".

There are, perhaps, basic limits to what we can know. Event if theories are developed, their application may be impossible because of the complexity of natural phenomena. Hawking is forced to concede: "... quantum mechanics enables us in principle to predict nearly everything we see around us within the limits of the uncertainty principle. In practice, however, the calculations required for systems containing more than a few electrons are so complicated that we cannot do them".[48] And this applies merely to the physical world; the biological one is orders of magnitude more complex.

Even if scientists claim that they have found a complete theory, Hawking admits that "we could never be quite sure that we had indeed found the correct theory, since theories can't be proved.[49] Even if a complete unified theory was developed and proved to be correct. Hawking states that "it would not mean that we would be able to predict events in general" because of "the limitation that the uncertainly principle of quantum mechanics sets on our powers of prediction". Further, he concedes that "we could not solve the equations of the theory exactly, except in very simple situations. We cannot even solve exactly for the motion of three bodies in Newton's theory of gravity, and the difficulty increases with the number of bodies and the complexity of the theory.[50]

All that is in the doubtful future. Today, science is unable to understand the complex global phenomena being brought about by the pollution Western technology has itself created. Nature is so complex that scientists cannot even predict the results of a simple stir in a tea cup. Climatologists half-jokingly suggest that a butterfly fluttering in Tokyo can theoretically trigger a tornado in Texas. It is not a matter of bigger and faster computers to do more calculations. New scientific discoveries have shown that in complex systems, small initial differences between two identical systems cause the systems to diverge rapidly. In such systems called chaotic—prediction of results becomes impossible because any input data measurement error causes calculations to go hopelessly wrong.

There may be inherent limitations to Western science's ability to study all interconnections with the environment, even if it had the will to do so: the ignorance results from the very methods of Western science. The microfragment of the universe that it isolates for laboratory study is disconnected from the rest of the universe and the latter, much larger, part of reality is ignored. In the case of studies where even bits and pieces cannot be brought into the lab, as in the case of climatology, programmed models are run on computers. In the process of isolating or modeling, what is not known and understood is automatically excluded. Unexpected effects are bound to turn up when the technology moves from laboratory to reality.

Hawking admits that "[i]f everything in the universe depends on everything else in a fundamental way, it might be impossible to get close to a full solution by investigating parts of the problem in isolation".[51] Western science, therefore, can never guarantee the accuracy of any the partial "solutions" it offers.

There is also the question of time. We still do not know what the exact long-term effects of pollution will be for the simple reason that only long-term studies can show them, while theory may not. And such studies are extremely expensive since they must go on indefinitely. However, the demands of paymasters for papers, patents and profits, results in precipitate and reckless interventions, a basic consequence of Western science's symbiosis with the industrial system.

The situation is made more obvious when effects accumulate over thousands of years. A science-fiction story tells about a respected journalist in a country that had a benevolent government, that was at peace internally and externally. He went on a holiday excursion in a Time Machine. Before they embarked on the journey, the guide warned the passengers that on no account were they to get off the Machine when they went back in time. But one of them, in his excitement at seeing dinosaurs, fell and killed a little butterfly. When they returned in time, they found that their country was now a police state ruled by a despot, at war with its neighbours. The journalist was arrested immediately he stepped out of the Time Machine.

Now Western technology is going over nature with the equivalent of millions of bulldozers. Western science promotes the delusion that all such actions have no long-term effects, or that they are somehow benign or neutral or average out. But every intervention must produce irreversible changes, changes which are not limited to entropy increase alone.

Western science believes that unless hypotheses are checked with experiments, they have little or no value. So no decisions on action need to be taken on suspect interventions until there is clear proof of harmful consequences. Such proof requires the actual occurrence of a statistically significant number of Chernobyls, and of deaths due to radiation-induced illnesses, before nuclear reactors are accepted as harmful. It requires the global climate to change measurably before steps to prevent it from changing can be recommended. Or worse, it requires the harmful effects of global climatic change to become evident before such change is accepted as harmful. Reality must be damaged—and perhaps even destroyed—before it is considered "scientific" to propose action to avoid damage.

One of the fundamental assumptions of Western science is that all experiments are repeatable. But when any action is taken, the real world changes. We cannot see what would have happened if that activity was avoided. We do not have "control" worlds with which to compare. Perhaps, this is why the extensive damage to the environment goes unnoticed or appears normal to most people, including scientists. What would be the state of the world today if just one product, explosives, had not been invented? What would be the state of the world today if Western science had not developed in such a gross manner?

The interventions that are causing global warming, the ozone hole, oceanic pollution, are experiments with the earth as a whole—experiments with the "lab", not merely in the lab. Scientists can also "blow up the lab", and not only are there no spare "labs" to experiment with, there could be no experimenters left. Our one and only "lab" may not be blowing up now, but it is certainly disintegrating rapidly. Western science ignores this with an obstinate optimism based on ignorance and arrogance.

With the imminent possibility of global climatic change and its potentially disastrous consequences, a few scientists are supporting the "precautionary principle". Such action indicates that science can no longer be taken as the sole or even the most important authority in making decisions that visibly affect people. But with science dependent on industry and governments only concerned with economic growth, there is no change of the principle being widely used.[52] Moreover, the scientists recommend the principle only because the consequences might be irreversible; this cannot be a guiding principle for protecting the environment.

The misuse of science is dismissed as an irrational aberration, but most of the applications of Western science and technology today are irrational. When there is so much uncertainty, rationality requires that we choose the safer path. A person who takes irresponsible risks bordering on suicide, is judged to be insane. Western scientists should not be excluded from this category when they behave in a similar manner. Those who work on nuclear weapons, those who create dangerously polluting chemicals, those who are recklessly rushing to produce genetically manipulated organisms, are all suicidal. But so are those who work on any product that contributes to global warming, which includes practically all of Western technological products because of their energy content. The ultimate irrationality consists of contributing to humanity's destruction when it is motivated by a search for "truth".

Another—perhaps fatal—problem arises in that once knowledge is obtained and disseminated, it is not easily undiscovered and withdrawn. Once the technogenie is out of the bottle it is difficult to put it back. Even if scientists now decide to stop work on the science that has led to harm, what has been done could still lead to more injury. Humanity will have to live with the bomb and biotechnology's products for ever. It's as impossible to be sure that there will be no lunatic in the years ahead to press the button or to release dangerous organisms as it is to prove any other universal negative.

Jonathan Schell points out: "It is the crowning irony of this lopsided development of human abilities that the only means in sight for getting rid of the knowledge of how to destroy ourselves would be to do just that—in effect, to remove the knowledge by removing the knower."[53]

Western science's theories may be internally valid

but sustainability requires a higher, holistic rationality which Western science is unable to provide and which it even claims is unnecessary. The answer to Bertrand Russell's question seems to be that Western scientific society cannot continue to exist.

THE QUESTION OF ETHICS

Mendelssohn states that domination is inherent in Western science and would be automatically available to anyone who develops such a science. "Using her (sic) superior technological potential against China, and later in Southeast Asia and the Pacific, Japan demonstrated the obvious fact that domination of less developed nations simply stems from the employment of this power . . . The Japanese example conclusively shows that, once the armoury created by natural philosophy is at hand, domination tends to follow. . . . Science and technology in the hands of man (sic)—and this means any man who has their use—confer on him an unprecedented degree of power over his neighbours. It appears that mankind has so far not found the means or the moral strength to resist the temptation of domination of man over man."[54]

While Japan failed in its attempt during the 1942-46 war to achieve a "Greater East Asia Co-Prosperity Sphere" by military means, it has succeeded, through technology-dependent economic exploitation, in gaining hegemony over practically the whole world. It is so much simpler when "enemies" are compelled, by unjust terms of trade, to invite you to destroy their forests, to permit you to run highly polluting industries in their fragile ecosystems and to pay handsomely for obsolete technology.

While Mendelssohn blames a lack of moral development for the inability to control Western science, it was that science itself which claimed that its rationality required no external ethical systems. Without the whole then-existing ethical base being weakened or co-opted, Western science perhaps would not have been able to grow at all. By diminishing and destroying all other moral structures, Western science furnished the licence, as well as the means, to dominate the rest of humanity. And this authorization has been freely used by those inclined and eager to exploit. In a similar manner, Western science has given the West the tools and the sanctions to consume and annihilate Nature.

Western scientists claim that their search for objective truth provides a strict code of ethics. "Understanding the universe" is a sufficient criterion for judging whether or not they should work on a particular topic. But the social and environmental consequences of their interventions are not considered "truth". Fermi, when confronted with the possible consequences of atomic bombs, said: "Do not bother me with your conscientious scruples! After all, the thing's superb physics."[55] Super sin is sanctified by "superb" science. Thus do they exonerate themselves from all liability for what they do.

No doubt some scientists are interested in knowledge for its own sake, but their results are quickly appropriated by the commercial or military systems over which they have no control. Politicians and militarists did not make nuclear weapons all by themselves. Einstein was supposed to be a peace-loving and gentle person, yet the whole of the nuclear arms industry has been built up on the basis of his theories. The Russell-Einstein Declaration, issued in 1955, imploring politicians to avoid war as a means of settling disputes, was blithely ignored by the military and political systems. Was this because the Declaration shows a singular lack of repentance and regret for the role that scientists played in developing weapons that "threaten the continued existence of mankind (sic)"?

Where does one draw the line of moral responsibility separating those who were culpable for the production and consequences of nuclear weapons and those who were not? At Oppenheimer, at Sakharov, at Fermi, at Einstein, at Rutherford, at Becquerel, at Lise Meitner? Western science gives unconditional absolution to all. But is it morally right for a scientist to carry on such work knowing that her/his results would surely be appropriated for the production of greater violence?

Biotechnology has now eliminated the need for nuclear weapons which have become too embarrassing for their owners and advocates Genetically engineered pathogens are being developed that will destroy the "enemy's" crops, livestock or population, without anyone being able to identify the responsible aggressor. Western scientists cannot resist the temptation to show how clever they are, with their proposals to develop and produce cheap and tempting new weapons of an endless variety.

Simpler technologies produce ethical problems, too. Chemists do not attach caveats when they produce a new chemical even though they are well aware that all its toxic effects can never be known.

Some Western scientists say that unless there is a balance between risk and reward, no progress can be made. They abuse statistics by claiming, for instance, that only one in a million is "at risk" because of a single radioactive or toxic pollutant. Little is known about the harmful effects of even one substance, let alone potent cocktails of them. With hundreds of such toxins acting simultaneously and perhaps synergistically, the chances of getting ill for a particular individual increases dramatically. And if that individual dies, she/he is murdered. But innocence is claimed because the violent effects are separated from their causes, remote and distant in space and time.

The problem of what genetically-modified and transgenic creatures should and should not be "created" and released into the environment is a complex one. While scientists claim that patenting of animals should be permitted but not human beings, where does one place the mouse with a human oncogene or a pig with a human gene that promotes growth? No matter how careful biotechnologists are in preventing their chimeras from getting loose in the environment, there will always be arrogant leaders like George Bush who will order their bombers to destroy the "enemy's" biotech laboratories.

The intimate connections between Western science, the military establishment and industry and the ethical consequences of such symbiosis were explicitly revealed during the Gulf war unleashed by Bush. The "surgical accuracy" of the latest high-technology weapons was displayed on global TV almost instantaneously and with it was shown the mass civilian deaths and destruction it produced. The cooperating media made such carnage seem normal and even good. The super power that the US's technology provided, enabled that country to ram through UN resolutions which were patently unjust. It was obvious that the purpose of the whole exercise was to protect its sources of oil, on which the whole economy of the West depends.

Those "defence" industries which developed such technology gloated. The Hughes Corporation produced a glossy little booklet, Winning the War, Striving for Peace, outlining the role of its technology in the Persian Gulf. "At no time in history have the military men and women of the nation—and their technology—performed so flawlessly," it boasts on the cover.[56]

That war provided an unprecedented opportunity for testing US weapons and strategy. Earlier, those who worked on such technology of mass death used computer simulations to test their technologies in war "games". These made death familiar and normal, and helped scientists to dissociate themselves and their research from reality. One American general claimed that he was very angry to have been misquoted. He never said that the end of life on the planet was acceptable. He was making the obvious point that 500 million dead was an acceptable level of casualties.[57]

Western science claims that it eliminates the need for religions, but Western science itself requires belief without proof. It is not merely that incomplete theories require one to swallow more than six impossible things before breakfast every day. The basic postulates of any science are unprovable and are, in effect dogmas to be taken on pure faith. Western science's claim to be able to know how the universe "works" is also an article of faith. It further proclaims that it can provide a high level of consumption for everyone although we live in a limited environment, and that its methods enable it to solve all problems arising from this. Such beliefs are plainly superstitious.

Because of its inherent contradictions, the practice of Western science necessarily requires immense, absolute faith. Science is idolised as the supreme good. It becomes more fanatic than other religions with its insistence that only through it can earthly salvation be achieved. This is the irrationality of total faith in reduced and restricted rationality.

Western science uses the "miracles" of technology to induce such absolute faith in "laypersons". But the "miracles" are turning out to be illusions and other means must be used. Language becomes an instrument of power. Jargon allows the mystified, sacred knowledge of the scientist-priests to be kept out of the hands of the laity. The ex-laboratory pronouncements of some of our scientists, particularly in the nuclear establishment, are to be accepted as blindly as ex-cathedra religious statements, but with this essential difference: people have the freedom to accept or reject the latter, while the consequences of Western science are imposed on all of us.

The search for Western scientific knowledge looks like a pure and noble striving but it has become a total, obsessive desire for domination that supplants all external ethical considerations. We can carry out Western scientific research and develop or use Western technology only if we make, unconsciously perhaps, a Mephistophelean pact to exchange a little bit of our souls for each little bit of Western science and technology.

11

Liberation Science & Technology

A liberative science and technology should be able to provide the basic material necessities for all human beings for an indefinite period. It should be intrinsically more sustainable and less damaging to the environment, it should be inherently incapable—or less capable—of being used for injustice. It should enable human beings to decide their own destiny within environmental resource constraints.

LIBERATION TECHNOLOGY

Our traditional technology and science has been and still is more liberative than the Western system.

Traditional technologies are not merely sets of techniques handed down from generation to generation. "Traditional" does not mean "obsolete", neither does it imply absolute good. It is the traditional methods of research, development, dissemination and use that are relevant, not necessarily all brought forward pieces of knowledge.

Since such research is constantly being carried out today, often in advance of or at the same time as formal, institutional research, a current example may help reveal the differences between institutional and traditional methods.

Since 1987, Warli Adivasis have been catching fish in nallas by stupefying them with the seeds of dandavan, Acacia auriculiformis. This Australian tree was first introduced into the Warli area around 1985. It takes about two years to flower and fruit, so the Adivasis' research has been carried out very quickly indeed.

A paper on the effects of extracts of this plant on fish was published in "Environment & Ecology" in 1988. The research required submission of project reports and budgets, a well-equipped laboratory, two species of "experimental" fish confined to aquaria, two "qualified" scientists who carried out the research, their guides, supporting staff from clerks to cleaners and accountants to administrators, large salaries, and a lot of time spent by all concerned. This type of research is carried out for its citation and commercial values, and for the degrees, employment and other benefits it provides scientists. For such scientists, the "outside" world exists merely as a source of raw materials for research—it has little value or needs of its own. Even in the extremely unlikely case of the published paper being read by Warlis, the information would be worthless to them, since the plants and the fish are identified by their botanical and zoological names only, and those particular fish species do not occur in the Warli area anyway.

Even though the theme of the institutional scientists' research was basically relevant to the people, the methods of Western science and the institutional structures make it inaccessible to them. In order to be put to practical use, the laboratory experiments would need to be repeated for the numerous different fish species all over the country with the local plants of each area. the results would then have to be communicated to millions of people.

The Warli research required no submission of budgets and reports, no elaborate establishment, no requisitions for apparatus and consumables, and was tested on the fish that need to be caught, in their natural environment. Warlis already use several plants for this purpose, so the research may have been done purely out of scientific curiosity or because the plants used earlier have disappeared, with the forests being replaced with monocultares of dandavan. The new knowledge has already diffused so widely that it has not been possible to trace who exactly did the research.

The need for recognition did not arise since what the innovative Warlis did was nothing extraordinary —it was what many of them normally do, what their culture expects and encourages them to do. The researchers felt no urge to write a paper, submit it for publication, wait for it to be published and for people to read, cite and applaud it. When they are appropriate, traditional technologies spread without "extension experts" and "modern" methods of communication. The Warlis' research may not be cited in any "learned" journal but their knowledge has already benefited many. And those who did the research, exercised their creativity and thus enhanced their self-worth and that of their community.

In another instance, Warlis use a wild, fast-growing nitrogen-fixing plant, Sesbania bispinosa, as a green manure for paddy, by sowing it in paddy fields at the first rains and ploughing it in within three weeks, just before transplantation. It provides sufficient nitrogen for the crop. A similar method was later discovered by "highly qualified" scientists at the vast establishment of the International Rice Research Institute (IRRI) in the Philippines. They used an African species, Sesbania rostrata, which required irrigation for six months before being ploughed in.

In sum, the main characteristics of traditional technology are: the technology is researched and developed by "ordinary" people, at little cost, perhaps without theories to support it. The innovators do not require formal recognition for their work. The technology uses local and usually low cost resources, and is of immediate relevance to the people. Others are free to use the technology and improve upon it. Knowledge is disseminated free and it spreads spontaneously by traditional oral means of communication. The processes of innovation as well as use are supported by traditional culture. Such a system cannot be easily used for domination; innovators do not achieve positions of power or authority because of their innovations, neither can the technology be "enclosed" by patents. The time when the innovation was made—centuries ago or today—or the continuing use of the technology is not of importance.

The traditional system encouraged self-reliance, thereby freeing people from the need to be dependent—and dominated—by others. Traditional technology allowed people the freedom to exercise their creativity to solve their own problems, to have control over their environment. Traditional technologies were mostly based on renewable raw materials, including sources of energy, making them sustainable.

Not all these criteria may be applicable to particular technologies and there may be other criteria that could be applicable, too.

What is known as "appropriate technology" usually does not satisfy these conditions.

The Extent of Peoples' Research

Much of traditional research has been based on the uses of plants for food, manures, pesticides, fodder, medicine, timber and other housing material, oil for cooking and lighting, cosmetics, dyes, tans, fibres, fuel, material for mats, baskets, ornaments, and dozens of other purposes.

Each experiment done by a person-in-the-field is small in itself, but when one considers the vast number of species of plants and the multiple uses to which each has been put, it can be seen that a tremendous amount of systematic, directed, conscious research and development has been undertaken by millions of normal people over millennia, resulting in a rich fund of knowledge.

Taking medicinal uses alone, if one multiplies the number of species of common plants in India (say, ten thousand), by the number of parts of a plant (the leaves, flowers, fruits, seeds, stem bark, roots, root bark and others) that are used, by the number of common diseases and other health uses for which each of these are tested (say a hundred, ranging from headaches to fertility control) and by the methods of preparation and dosages possible, one gets a faint idea of the stupendous amount of research that has been accomplished. If one takes into account the possible synergistic combinations of herbs, this is increased by several orders of magnitude.

Attempts to systematically collect this information were made by the British in the last century. One—rather incomplete—result was George Watt's "A Dictionary of the Economic Products of India", published in 1897, which ran to ten volumes. Much of their contents is concerned with the medicinal uses of plants.

While it is well known that a colossal number of traditional technological practices have been developed over the centuries in India and other regions, it is usually believed that the use of most of these has died out because of the onslaught of Western technologies and science. However, investigations have shown that not only are these technologies still widely employed among "primitive" Adivasis but also that they are widespread among non-Adivasis, in rural as well as urban areas. This is extensively so in the fields of agriculture and herbal medicine, but is also fairly prevalent in most other areas as well.

It is also believed that further research is not being carried out which encourages the nation that traditional technology is static. The fact that innumerable uses have been found by "ordinary" people for almost all the exotic plants which have recently been introduced into the country shows that research is still being continuously and widely carried out.

The work of Anil Gupta and his team at the Centre for Management in Agriculture, Indian Institute of

Management, Ahmedabad, is particularly revealing. They have carried out a systematic collection of farmers' innovative practices and published their results in a number of papers as well as in a journal. Honey Bee. The number of such practices collected is amazing, showing clearly that the innovative process is still active and thriving.

There are evidently many more scientists working outside, rather than within, institutional laboratories. The former conduct research in their daily life, while carrying on their normal occupations, in their fields and homes, using locally available resources. Such a technology is naturally concerned with the provision of vital necessities, not with the wants of professional scientists. It is what the majority of people in the world still depend on for their survival.

The traditional scientific method evidently will not allow one to work on high energy particle physics, gene transfer technology or micro-electronics. The local sciences do not know the "realities" of quarks and quasars but they have certainly been successful in surviving and thriving in regionally closed environments.

Formal Vs Peoples' Research

The importance of such research can be determined by asking whether the research done so far could have been carried out in formal institutions, and if so, what its cost would be, and who would actually benefit from it.

Pharmaceutical companies claim that they spend millions of dollars on developing each drug that they manufacture and that it takes over a decade to research and produce each one. Costing at similar rates would value the research carried out traditionally at trillions of dollars. The appropriation of our traditional herbal knowledge must accordingly be saving the pharmaceutical companies billions of dollars and centuries of time, without compensation for their use of our intellectual property, of course.

The chemicals of less than 1% of all plant species have been studied by Western science, while nearly all plants in India have multiple uses based on their chemicals. The percentage of plant species studied will, no doubt, increase rapidly through Western research as well as by the extinction of unstudied species by habitat destruction. But the requirement of identifying the chemical prior to using plant materials ensures that the Western system will take a very long time before it finds uses for all plant species, even if Western scientists continue to use our heritage to guide them.

Much of such formal research is also pointless, since it works by isolating and checking single plant chemicals in vitro or in clinical tests. These can easily produce false-negative results, since each plant contains numerous chemicals—neem, for instance, has more than a hundred identified compounds—each of which acts in several ways. And working with all possible synergistic combinations would take still longer.

It is obvious that the Western scientific method could not have led to the discovery of the multitude of uses to which Indian plants have been put, and that formal scientists will have a tough job keeping up with people's research. As an example, Warlis already use dandavan for medicinal purposes while allopathic medicine does not.

It is correctly claimed that many Indian formal scientists merely repeat research that has already been carried out in the West. But it is highly amusing to watch the frantic research that is being done in the West and here, which merely replicates what has been researched here hundreds of years ago. Pharmaceutical and pesticide multinationals have established elaborate laboratories merely to study traditional practices. Individual scientists want to be the first to "discover" what has already been discovered ages ago—in an intellectual analogy to Columbus' "discovery" of America. The vast accumulation of indigenous knowledge now supplies numerous themes for doctoral dissertations, with such stolen research being considered scientifically proper. A number of papers deal with efforts to "verify" traditional uses of plants, though only a few cite such use. Practically none can credit the first researcher, it being strangely assumed that it is valid to appropriate anonymous discoveries. Some that do cite traditional use, arrogantly end with "this confirms folkloric practice", although such practice is scientific, not "folkloric", and self-confirming. Hardly any of the papers disprove traditional knowledge and such negative results could be due to the reductionist methods used.

It is becoming increasingly obvious that a centralised research establishment cannot solve the multitude of agricultural problems requiring resolution in minutely differing ecological niches. Centralised research, by its very nature, cannot work in microniches; farmers work at the few hundred square metre level. Even if agricultural scientists carry out their experiments in the field, the conditions may be vastly different from the conditions in which particular farmers would use the technology.

For many years scientists at IRRI believed that they would be able to develop paddy varieties—arrogantly numbered from IR8 on—which they would supply to the whole rice-growing world. They have now made the discovery that, besides being susceptible to pests and having other problems, "standard" varieties cannot produce well because of local variations in climate, soil and so on. IRRI has given up promoting "universal" varieties and is now distributing germplasm through the various regional rice research centres. But neither can regional centres produce varieties to suit all microniches. So we are full circle back to the need for traditional varieties selected by millions of small farmers. However, there is a new danger lurking on the horizon. The demand by the West for patent rights on new species is an attempt to stop all on-farm research.

Centralised agricultural research is expensive and negligible compared to decentralised, on farm, by farmer, research. It takes more than a decade to check out a new fruit species and costs thousands of rupees to do so in a horticultural establishment. How much would it cost and how many millennia would it take if such research centres had been required to develop all the varieties of mangoes that we already have?

The need for millions of local experimenters is made essential and urgent by the possibilities of global warming and the destruction of the ozone layer. It is impossible to predict the innumerable changes that may occur in millions of microniches. A centralised research system would have to collect data from each locality, work out alternatives and feed back the results to the corresponding region, even while the environmental conditions may have changed during institutional scientists' struggles with bureaucracy. On the other hand, local research could provide millions of correct solutions faster and continuously. The problem of transferring technology from laboratories to field users can be avoided simply by transferring the research back to the field.

Western scientists claim that what is being done by people is not true science because there is no elaborate theoretical foundation. No doubt, those two scientists knew exactly the structure of the saponins and how they stupefy fish, and this knowledge could be used to identify other plants which could also serve to catch fish. But people's knowledge already covers hundreds of such plants, growing in every corner of the country.

Moreover, theories have been highly developed in the fields of health, for instance, in India. There may have been theories in other fields which could be lost. Such theories may or may not have been rational in the Western scientific sense; much of traditional technology could have developed from a recognition of patterns in phenomena. Mathematisation is unnecessary and may even be impossible in such cases. This is particularly so when a large number of environmental interactions have to be taken into account.

An important corollary of development by the people is that the technology is invented and tested in the field, where all natural interactions, known and unknown, are allowed to play their part. It is holistic in practice and thereby avoids the pitfalls of incomplete and incorrect theories. India's vast accumulation of traditional technology would probably not have developed had people waited for detailed theories to explain all that they discovered. If innovators had restricted their experiments to those based on logic or patterns, it is possible that many experiments would not have been carried out at all and that much knowledge left undiscovered.

Most of the current research by farmers appears to be of the trial and error type. Herbal medicinal research seems to be so, too, though examples of patterns of cause and effect were observed and used. Practical experimentation on a vast scale must have been carried out much before any of the ayurvedic theories could have developed.

Some of those patterns are now helping Western science. The testing of thousands of plants for use for several diseases should result in plants which have the same chemicals being used for exactly the same set of diseases. Some species of Plumbago, called "chitrak", have been widely used in medicine for centuries. An ayurvedic practitioner brought to the attention of a botanist that their medicines used are exactly the same as those of some species of Drosera—the insectivorous sundew plants—which are not used much because they are rare. These species are also called "chitrak", although they belong to a plant family different from the Plumbago one. It has now been found that these sundews have the same active anthraquinone, plumbagin, as the Plumbago species. Plumbagin is not common in other plants, and the botanist noticed that many of the plants that did have it, were insectivorous, leading him to suspect that the Plumbago species may also be insectivorous. On examination, he found a number of dead insects on the glandular hairs of their calyces, which appears to confirm his hypothesis.[58]

Theories could also possibly limit research and use. Take, for instance, the use of rui (Calotropis gigantea) leaves as a green manure. The leaves have very low quantities of nitrogen, potassium and phosphorus and if it had been explained to farmers that green manures are good because of these chemicals, they would not have used rui at all. But they use it widely and it is evidently effective in improving crop productivity—probably because of its pesticidal or nematicidal effects.

Creativity involves breaking set rules or patterns of thought or finding new rules or contradictions in old ones. Has the enormous traditional creativity been based on the fact there are few if any rules at all?

As Gandhi said: every man must be his own scientist and every village a science academy. Anyone has the—and everyone should exercise the right—to be a "scientist" or "technologist", to develop new technologies or to modify old ones. There appears to be no need for a separate class of people who do only or mainly such work. Those who develop traditional practices are mainly—but not necessarily those who use the practices themselves. There are few specialist boundaries. The same farmers develop botanical pesticides, herbal treatments for their bulls, methods of catching fish and many other practices.

Western science has diminished traditional creativity by removing research and development from the public domain, by privatising and commercialising it. The impression has been created that no one except self-labeled "highly qualified scientists" do research. Shifting science from the villages to the laboratories—the enclosure of the scientific commons—appears to have been the initial means of controlling knowledge. When "experts" claim to be the sole repositories of knowledge, the rest of humanity is deemed to be "ignorant", and much of the rest of Western humanity has internalised this notion. Parallel with this process, goes the transfer of power from people in general to the self-elected "elite". These try to devalue the science of those in the field, dismissing it as chance findings and superstition. The Adivasis, particularly, are called ignorant, even by those who appropriate their knowledge under the guise of ethno—sciences. Such appropriation, in fact, confirms the validity of traditional sciences—if such proof is required.

Socially Appropriate & Sustainable Technology

Traditional technologies are seen to be more appropriate than Western ones if criteria of social justice and permanence are used. Social justice requires that all the peoples of the earth have an equal right and access to the resources of the earth; permanence requires that all future generations—an indefinite number of them—have the same rights, too. With resources—including the resource of pollution sinks—limited to those on a closed planet, the Western system, based as it is on hyper-consumption of non-renewable resource fostered by its technology, is inherently unsustainable and unjust. Liberation technologies contribute to sustainability and justice, since they use only renewable resources or non-renewable ones in a manner which make them recyclable. They require a minimum of energy for their production and use, and all that energy comes from renewable sources, mainly renewable power, human or other animal.

Traditional technologies are of immediate relevance to the people in the region in which they are developed. They are rarely—if at all—invented merely for the sake of the knowledge gained or the technology itself. Farmers may develop a botanical insecticide because a pest has attacked their crops, or artisans may develop a new plant-derived dye for the cloth they weave. Institutional entomologists, chemists, veterinarians and other specialists usually do not use the techniques they develop directly for their own sustenance. Their main purpose is to publish and patent, though there may be exceptions, but these exceptions are working against the rules of the system rather than with them.

Traditional technologies are usually low in cost, since they have to be affordable by village artisans and farmers. The Western industrialised system, on the other hand, develops technology mainly for big farmers and industrial capitalists, where the higher the cost, the larger the profits usually made by the manufacturers.

Traditional technologies mainly use locally available materials and renewable ones, plant and animal products growing in the neighbourhood. Metals are used but usually in a form that makes them long-lasting and recyclable. However, plants that do not grow in the locality may be imported from distant places as, for instance, dye and herbal plant products. Western technology is almost always based on raw materials brought from distant sources consuming enormous quantities of fossil fuels; Its products are affordable only because the fuels are priced at absurdly low levels and pollution costs are externalised. This alone makes it unsustainable.

The fact that most of people's technology is limited to what is obtained from plants and animals is seen by the Westernised as a major defect, but this is the only possible basis for a truly sustainable society. All people have been and are presently dependent on plants and animals, not only for food but for many industrial products, too. This dependence, foolishly concealed now, will become more obvious and increasingly important as fossil resources start running out.

Most of traditional technology is inherently socially appropriate, whereas exploitation is intrinsic even in apparently beneficial Western technology. As long as irrigation was carried out using water drawn from surface wells by animal power, there were limits to how much groundwater a farmer could extract. But bore-hole drilling manses, deepwell pumps and engines to run them, have allowed rich farmers to deplete groundwater, thus drying out the surface wells of those who cannot afford such technology. Such inherently exploitative technology requires social control if equity is to be served, while the simpler technology does not. Moreover, the "high" technology is not sustainable and leads to its self-elimination when the groundwater is entirely exhausted or when saline water seeps in.

Traditional systems have intrinsic social and environmental feedback. When people live in a region from which they would not normally emigrate, they are extremely careful to avoid damaging their environment to the point of unsustainability. When interventions are made in such an environment, any deterioration is usually quickly observed and further intervention of that type avoided. The development of traditional technologies is limited to those which do not pollute the environment, exhaust resources or produce unemployment. It could be that the "failure" to develop labour-displacing textile machinery in India was due to precisely such social control. It is only because the Western system promotes the ravaging of remote regions that it can temporarily prolong its unsustainability. However, there were aberrations brought about by local exploitation and some traditional technologies could have long-term harmful effects.

The Dissemination of Traditional Technologies

Traditional technologies spread by the demonstration effect and by oral communication. A particular technology may diffuse to a few neighbours only or far and wide across whole regions. An innovation may have been developed for the particular ecological conditions where it originated, or by an artisan in a widespread industry. On the other hand, innovations which do not work may not spread at all or quickly fall into disuse if disseminated. Those who are interested in using a particular practice can get full details of raw materials, equipment and processes from the innovator or from the person from whom they have learned about the practice. The technologies are not covered by anything corresponding to patent or intellectual property rights which could possibly limit their dissemination.

Against this, an institutional innovation normally requires publication in one of a limited number of "reputed"—preferably foreign—journals before it can be disseminated. And very often, the technology does not reach those who need to use it. Further barriers to its free use are introduced by patenting the technology. Moreover, most published papers do not give full details of how the practice is to be actually used, neither are the authors available for consultation—without charge. However, in some fields such as agriculture and animal husbandry, the extension services provided by many research institutions do disseminate research results without or before publication. But wherever technology has been commercialised, aggressive salesmanship is required for its profitable dissemination.

Because of the fast erosion of traditional knowledge, it is essential to record as much as possible before it dies out. Even more important, is the need for informing others that people's research is going on today and that they can do it too. The collected data, therefore, requires dissemination, through journals which reach farmers and artisans. A good examples of this is the Honey Bee, mentioned earlier. The journal is being produced in several Indian languages so that the innovator's themselves can read about their work, comment on it if wrongly reported and gain confidence to keep alive and healthy the traditional research system. There is an urgent need for similar journals that cover other areas of liberation technology. These examples are published without any institutional "peer review", though the interpretation of some of these practices by institutional scientists has also been published and, perhaps, peer reviewed.

However, publishing such data makes it more accessible to those who wish to commericalise it. Westernised scientists learn about traditional technologies in our publications, make slight modifications and then patent them, perhaps even preventing the originators of the technology from using it themselves.

Recognition & Rewards for Innovation

Knowledge is freely disseminated, as seen in the case of the use of dandavan for catching fish. This is true altruistic behaviour, since such dissemination could reduce the quantity of fish caught by the innovator since others would be using the technology in the same region in the same ponds and nallas.

The satisfaction that innovators get from producing something new that works to improve their lives, as well as their community's appreciation that goes with it, appears to be enough of a reward; there is no compulsion to seek formal recognition by society at large. The community's informal recogni-tion could be innate in the culture which promotes traditional technology. Traditional innovators were and are satisfied with their own peer group appreciation of their creativity, the peer group of a farmer innovator being other farmers, his/her neighbours, friends, relatives, etc, who would in all probability use the technology. It is pressure from such people which possibly limits developments to socially and environmentally appropriate ones.

The peer group of formal scientists are the innovator's specialist colleagues, who are normally uninterested in its use at all and perhaps only concerned with the profits that they can make out of it. Since the rest of society has little control over the "experts", there are few social and environmental constraints on what research is carried out.

Traditional technologies are available free for use by others, with the innovators happy to see the use of their inventions spread without expectations of any financial recompense. This is an essential characteristic of the traditional system.

The formalisation of traditional knowledge does appear to lead to institutionalisation, for instance, the ayurvedic system and the Adivasi bhagat systems. Members of such institutions, though accepted as part of the traditional system, either charge for their services or expect to be recompensed in some way.

If the traditional system is commercialised, it may be destroyed completely, since innovators would tend to conceal their work until they were assured of financial recompense. The fact that the cash economy has penetrated nearly everywhere does not mean that the economic commons should be further enclosed.

Institutional scientists want and get financial rewards even if the innovation is of no immediate practical importance. Further financial compensation might be available if the innovation is patented and then used widely.

The Supporting Culture

A particular culture can be considered as a whole system of knowledge, of a way of understanding the complexity of the natural world so that rules can be laid down which lead to the preservation of that society. Such a culture effectively serves to maintain a production system that serves all its members while not endangering the environment. Culture determines what sort of knowledge is transmitted from generation to generation, which innovations are to be encouraged, to whom and how the accumulated and new knowledge has to be spread and puts restraints on its use.

Our traditional culture ensured that the technologies did not produce unemployment, did not overuse natural resources or pollute the environment and hence was sustainable. There was no value seen in the possession of an increasing quantity of material products or in a lifestyle that stressed comfort even at the cost of the environment and justice.

The Adivasi systems of knowledge are well known but the support given to innovation is not so visible. Adivasis are normally looked down upon and ridiculed by non-Adivasis in a village. The latter particularly go out of their way to laugh at any Adivasi who attempts to improve his/her framing or other traditional ways. Adivasis, therefore, rarely tell anyone outside their community of the experiments they undertake, with the result that outsiders think that they lack initiative and imagination as well as scientific curiosity. It is only when they gain confidence in the outsider from the latter's genuine desire to learn from them, that they relate their experiments. It then becomes evident that the community support for experimentation and the community appreciation for what they do has been strong enough to counter the negative forces which the aliens normally project.

That there was oppression within traditional technologies and that there is a much room for improvement, is acknowledged. The essential difference appears to be that Western culture has exploitation built into and hence inseparable from it, while some traditional cultures do not. Much misunderstanding results from the view that traditional cultures are or should be static archaeological museum pieces.

The traditional values which such cultures promoted need to be compared with the values of Westernised system. If the latter turn out to be different and, perhaps, even contradictory, then the traditional systems could disappear unless the latter's values are promoted, while the Westernised values are deprecated. The Westernised system and its values may itself be responsible for the destruction of much of the traditional systems over the last few centuries.

Preservation of the Traditional System

There is increasing discussion and action today on the collection of information on and preservation of traditional technologies still extant, on the revival of those that have fallen into disuse and on the present day relevance of traditional technologies compared to those of the West.

The continuing persistence of traditional technology and its revival now is a result of the

Westernised system being unable to solve the problems individual farmers or artisans face, since its so-called solutions are too expensive, damage the environment, produce unemployment and have other obvious defects. Further, the people are realising that the Westernised system is not interested in reaching them except for further exploitation, and that it is in fact dropping them out of the industrial employment system, particularly after the IMF-enforced liberalisation process was begun. These are the people who need technologies that will allow them to survive with dignity and this is where traditional technologies have an important role to play.

The educational, health and other Westernised sub-systems demean traditional systems. It is very noticeable that those Adivasis who have been through the formal educational system do not know the uses of dandavan and most other plants, and often cannot even recognise common species. It does not seem possible that the formal education system can replace the traditional transfer of knowledge from parents to children as well as between siblings, which is based on continuous observation and practice in the field.

The forest and other commons are also essential to the preservation of traditional technology. Knowledge can be lost when the base for its practice degenerates, for instance, when deforestation destroys the plants from which medicines and other products are obtained.

The West patents their "discoveries" based on our knowledge and uses them for further exploitation even while labeling our traditional knowledge as false and denying us intellectual property rights.

Such commercialisation has disastrous effects on our genetic resources. Sarpagandha (Rauvolfia serpentina) has been used here for thousands of years for treating cardiac and mental diseases with little reduction in the availability of the plants. But when allopathy began using it to produce the drug reserpine, the plant was collected on such a vast scale that it has disappeared from most of its natural habitat, with an immense loss of genetic diversity. This has happened with most of the plants used by the West to produce drugs. It seems likely to happen to plants like neem being currently commercialised for pesticide use.

The following quotation from an article in Scientific American reveals what is happening. [59] "The first neem-based commercial product has reached the market in the US. . . . The US Department of Agriculture has studied the tree since the early 1970s, and W. R. Grace & Company bought the rights to market a neem pesticide. . . . For now, W. R. Grace depends on a far-flung network, which sometimes begins with poor villagers in India who gather neem fruits that have fallen from trees lining the roadside to provide shade from the harsh sun. . . . With "green" products all the rage, though, Grace has had no trouble marketing its product. 'If I had a little more, I could sell more,' says F. Peter Boer, Grace's chief technical officer."

With the expansionist pressures of western culture on all other cultures, an urgent need is to minimise interference with traditional cultures, to allow them to develop on their own. It is often said by the westernised elite that they have no right to deny indigenous peoples entrance into the mainstream. A telling answer is provided by the

Warlis who live in the Borivali National Park within the city of Bombay, probably the most westernised city in India. They do not want to enter the mainstream, all they ask is to be left alone—which of course, the mainstream, in its generosity to share its "comforts", does not. We should not, therefore, arrogantly assume that we have the burden of preserving their culture, but we do need to ensure space for them to preserve it on their own.

The fact that western culture has spread and is spreading so far and wide is taken to be a sign of its superiority. But its success in overcoming other cultures is not necessarily a sign of excellence in other areas besides dominance, just as cancerous tumour's ability to spread is not seen to be a boon to the body in which it grows. Western culture has been diffused by the economic and political power that the West obtained from its science and technology.

There is also a vital need for people to support traditional practitioners by using their products in preference to those produced by unsustainable methods. Their existence will be vital to our survival when—not if—the non-sustainable Western system reaches its unavoidable limits.

LIBERATION SCIENCE

With the exception of the indigenous health systems which have a firm theoretical basis, traditional technology appears to be mostly empirical. However, it may appears so simple because it is not known how traditional experimenters operate: whether, for instance, they innovate purely at random or whether they have reasons for testing a particular plant for pest control or for medicinal use. Reports of traditional practices only rarely give such reasons, while reports of traditional innovations only mention those trials which have succeeded. Studying the failures could reveal more about how the experimenter thinks.

The concern is not with the Western scientific reason why the technology works but rather the "scientific" reasons, if there are any, why the experimenter chose a particular set of materials or processes in an attempt to solve a particular problem.

There may be no theoretical basis for the choices made by some of the experimenters at least. Plants, for instance, may be tested for pesticidal action just because they are available at the time a pest attacks the farmer's crop. It may be only those who have been trained in the Western scientific method who feel a need to have theories and who get intellectual satisfaction from them. Such theories could help in hastening research, a need which may arise because of rapidly changing global or local environmental conditions. But the moment this comes into play, it is a move away from a liberative to an institutional system, though one much improved over the unadulterated Western system. This difference is obvious in the health, field, where the institutionalised ayurvedic system has become distanced from the people, while the family herbal treatment system has remained a people's technology.

Whether or not scientific theorising occurs, in some cases or in all, much traditional technology apparently forms part of a larger knowledge system which is broad in outlook and which serves as a theoretical base for keeping the technology within the bounds of sustainability.

There are several such systems, from those of various Adivasi clans to the more formalised ones that have operated in India and still guide the conduct of many here. One such is the belief in a cosmic order, Rita, which "sees" everything, including human beings, as one integrated universe. This must be distinguished from "knowing all about reality" in that it accepts all of reality, without the need for theories of "everything". The emphasis is not upon comprehension beyond that fundamental proposition but on having criteria by which to judge actions. The ancient sages said that those who are unable to see this are the truly ignorant because they have incomplete knowledge. They also maintained that only the attainment of an absolute unity between humans and the universe would produce such awareness.

A belief in the existence of a cosmic order is an a priori assumption whose truth cannot be theoretically proved. But all human knowledge systems—including Western science—have to start with a priori assumptions. Western science's belief that there is an underlying order in the universe without which natural laws discovered on earth would not be applicable elsewhere and the search for such laws itself would be foolish, is also an a priori assumption.

Acting on a belief in a cosmic order contributes more to sustainability than the limited understanding that Western science provides. The earlier attitude has "worked" in the sense that it sustained life whereas Western culture with the science that it sponsored has led to a diminishing of planetary survival.

A belief in cosmic order embodies a respect for

all life and non-life. "Seeing" ourselves as one with the universe involves living in harmony with Nature, living in a manner that tries to preserve the integrity of the whole of creation. Harmony demands that we strive to protect all life forms since each has a right to exist and each contributes to the survival of all. Each individual is important, not merely the survival of the species for the sake of the commercial value of its genes. This then leads us to the old Indian principle of least interference.

Even if one does not believe in the existence of a cosmic order, an admission that, because of the immense complexity of natural systems, human understanding is necessarily limited constrains interventions in the environment to be made with utmost caution. Intervention needs to be minimised simply because the natural system is too complex to meddle with. Such an admission of the limitations of human knowing is itself alternative knowledge. The absence of particular theorising is not a deficiency of method, but an acknowledgment of the complexity of reality and the limitations of the human mind.

It may be claimed that a belief in minimising interference implies that natural systems develop or evolve optimally, but there is concern about the use of the word "optimum". The term may be taken to mean that ecological regions in which humans do not intervene evolve in directions which maximise the conversion of the resource available in that region into a diverse plant and animal biomass. On the other hand, it could also mean that most human interferences that go beyond the minimal, appreciably degrade the ecosystem and reduce its ability to survive under external stress. These statements cannot be confirmed, since the complexity of the systems do not allow us to check what exactly is being maximised and, in any case, natural systems are not static but have continuously changing species as well as mass.

The principle of least interference can also be derived from the evidence of resource degradation and environmental pollution. Deep ecologists in the West have arrived at this principle out of their belief that justice requires that all life on earth be respected. This principle appears to be the only basis on which a sustainable society can be established.

But this principle is rejected by the Western system, not with any rational justification, but on the grounds of impracticality, since it cannot provide the high levels of consumption for people who are assumed to be inherently greedy. The Western system thereby declares that pollution and resource depletion and ultimately the destruction of all life, are eminently "practical" and inevitable.

On the other hand, some have claimed that the Eastern philosophies cannot handle today's situations, since it was Western ecologists who first blew the whistle on recent environmental problems. Western scientists may have discovered these crises, but the crises resulted from their own science. They should not take credit for a rather belated perception of the dangers of their own system. Minimal interference would have prevented such degradation in the first place.

On the personal level, some eastern philosophies merely require one to simplify one's lifestyle, with personal example inducing others to follow. However, the rapidity with which the Western system is damaging the environment and the enormous existing and increasing injustice may require one to act to rectify the social and environmental situation. There is also a need to acquire knowledge of how to mesh ourselves with Nature, to reduce the harm done by our interventions to a minimum.

A couple of examples of where the principle of least interference may lead, may help.

It has taken decades for Western science to realise some of the harmful effects of DDT and other synthetic pesticides. A recent discovery is that pests which have developed resistance to DDT are also resistant to a whole range of the latest pesticides, since they are all targeted on only one insect organ. This appears to annul the whole of pesticide "science".

This has led to the Integrated Pest Management (IPM) method which uses biological pest control but does not exclude the use of synthetic pesticides. It requires formal scientists to identify pest types and quantify their damage. It needs the artificial multiplication of natural parasites and predators. It has been designed for commercialisation and control by "experts" and big business.

An example where establishment scientists have appeared to help is in the use of neem (Azadirachta indica) as a field pesticide. While neem has been used as a storage pesticide for centuries, the discovery of its specific antifeedant properties occurred in the early 1960's in the Indian Agricultural Research Institute, New Delhi. Since then, hundreds of scientists, most of them in the West, have worked on neem, and numerous papers have been published, which have shown that neem can be used effectively against a very large number of field pests. The use of neem and other botanical pesticides is only now being accepted as scientific because of such research. The evidence of centuries of effective use is dismissed on the grounds that there was no scientific basis before, even though it worked in practice. By contrast, synthetic pesticide technology is considered to be valid because the chemicals have been proved to be toxic to pests in laboratories, even though they may increase the numbers and varieties of pests in the field.

Neem and other botanical pesticides have a number of chemicals which act simultaneously on more than one physiological system of an insect. In order to develop resistance to botanicals, there would need to be several simultaneous mutations, and the probability of this happening is very low. Hence, their successful use for hundreds of years.

But Western scientists studying neem are doing so mainly for the purpose of identifying its active chemicals, extracting and purifying or synthesising them and commercialising their knowledge. The use of single chemicals from plants increases the probability of resistance developing serially as the pesticide industry selects and discards one neem chemical after another as insects develop further resistance. The use of "crude" extracts, prepared in a few minutes at practically no cost, is thus seen as a more "scientific" method of using neem.

Western scientists, supported by agribusiness, are now examining all the plants that have been researched and that have been or are being used for pest control by Indian and other traditional farmers. In the meantime, farmers are continuing their research—on what theoretical basis we do not know.

Those who promote IPM claim that biological pest control with the use of, for instance. Bacillus thuringiensis (Bt), is a step forward since the product is a "natural" toxin. However, several insects, such as diamondback moths in Hawaii and potato beetles in Florida, have developed resistance to Bt. Bt-resistant insects have also been found in Japan, the Philippines, Thailand and Taiwan.

The use of synthetic pesticides have turned many relatively harmless insects into new and nasty pests. The destruction of forests has led to insects, which lived off forest plant species, moving to neighbouring fields and attacking crops.

It appears, therefore, that insects and other organisms become pests when natural ecosystems are unbalanced by interference. Insects are not normally a problem if, for instance, traditional crop varieties and farming methods are used in a diverse plant and animal environment.

Moreover, the cultivation of crops itself is an intervention so perhaps there is a need to improve on traditional mixed cropping and rotational systems, with, for instance, agroforestry or even more complex systems approaching nearer to natural conditions.

The manufactures of the Bt insecticides now recommend that farmers use it sparingly, but merely so that its commercial life could be prolonged. In the meantime, transgenic Bt-producing crops such as cotton have been developed, and although not yet introduced for field use, may soon be. This could hasten the development of Bt-resistant insects. Recommendations are now being made that farmers should use crop rotations and cultivate "refuge" crops along field borders so that some Bt-susceptible insects could survive.[60] Western technologists are being compelled to move towards more natural conditions.

If we had started holistically, with minimal interference, perhaps all the intermediate steps could have been avoided.

Or take the problem of energy. The use of fossil fuel based energy requires scarce resources and is highly polluting, so renewable energy converters are seen as a solution. Crops are considered very poor converters of incident solar energy, since their efficiency is only about 1-3%. The efficiency of trees is higher at about 10%, since they do not have to start from seed each year, so agroforestry is an improvement.

Solar photovoltaic converters are said to be even better, giving an efficiency of about 20%, and much research is being done to improve them further. But, unlike photovoltaics, plants convert solar energy even at low light levels. Further, some plants have two (and perhaps more) types of photosynthetic pathways and automatically switch from one to the other, depending on the wavelengths of incident light available to them, when they are in direct sunlight and when they are in shade. Many plants are also phototropic, turning their leaves to maximise input, without the expensive mechanisms required to keep the solar converters similarly aligned. Moreover, the non-renewable energy and Resources that go into the manufacture, transport and maintenance of solar cells and their associated equipment are considerable. Plants, grown under organic conditions, need no such energy and raw materials and are fully recyclable. All these increase the comparative efficiency of plants.

Further, the efficiency figures are based on the calorific or fuel value of the plants, whereas plants also use some of that same few percent of solar energy to produce a wide range of complex chemicals. If the energy that would be required by industry to synthesise these chemicals were taken into account, the efficiency of plants would be seen to be enormously higher than those of photocells. For instance, plants, in symbiosis with microorganisms, use negligible energy to fix nitrogen, compared to that required by current synthetic processes.

It is then said that the process of isolating the plant chemicals and purifying them would also require energy, but such separation is mainly required for commercialisation. People's use as medicines and pesticides does not need isolation since "crude" extracts often work better than single purified chemicals.

But Western technologists are not interested in solar energy "devices" that can be used directly by the people free of cost. They are only concerned with energy converters which have to be bought or whose output can be metered. The "technology" of growing plants and using crude extracts is non-commercialisable.

Further, there are limits to the quantity of energy we can sustainably use. Even renewable plant resources can be depleted and the complete recycling of non-renewable resources will never be possible. Avoiding the exploitation of an infinite number of future generations requires minimal use of energy.

The search for a liberating science requires a holistic search for truth. Holism involves the study of all sciences—bodies of knowledge—from traditional to Western science.

The movement towards holistic thinking can occur in several phases. One step would involve merely breaking down the barriers between Western science's internal divisions, resulting in more interdisciplinary studies. Another step goes beyond the boundaries of Western science and takes account of all the interactions with the economic, social and natural environmental systems. In still another, the understanding that Western rationalism is merely one method of obtaining knowledge among many liberates us to use other means of acquiring knowledge and other systems of knowledge.

Holism encompasses knowledge of false knowledges or incomplete knowledges. It requires the rational study of irrationality, since irrationality must be accepted as a valid human condition. Holism includes cultural support and constraint, which may appear to be irrational according to Western thinking, but which control individual or group selfishness for the sake of the whole.

Such studies should reveal the limitations of each method of obtaining knowledge and of each existing knowledge system. But holism's aim is not to poke holes in existing knowledge systems; its study must lead to action towards building a just, sustainable society. Assumptions of order and unity could lead to a different understanding, to universal laws for guiding action but without a mathematical basis since mathematics cannot deal with life processes, ethics and justice.

Holistic thinking may be considered speculation or dogma because proof can only come from the continuing survivability of a system based on these principles. On the other hand, proof of Western science's invalidity is increasing daily as its inherent unsustainability is exposed. Final, definitive proof of its irrationality can only come when it destroys all of us.

Living in an Unjust World

What is discussed above is an ideal situation and while ideals can provide criteria by which those who are concerned about justice and sustainability can judge their actions, we are all immersed in an unjust society on which we depend even for our sustenance.

Holism accepts that establishment scientists cannot immediately renounce Western science and all its works, neither can we instantly discard all the technology which ensnares us. Most of us, whether scientists or not, have to earn our living in an unjust milieu, surviving on an expropriated surplus. Jobs that wholly contribute to justice are very rare. Few have the knowledge and the skills to sustain themselves on the production of basic necessities. But we can continuously reduce our unjust dependence and contribute more to furthering justice.

The role that Westernised scientists can play in the promotion of traditional technology needs to be examined. Scientists can try to interpret traditional practices, both old and recent, using Western science. However if the results of their interpretation confirm the usefulness of the practice, the traditional system is strengthened, and the innovator—if she/he is aware of such confirmation—will be encouraged to continue innovating. If on the other hand, the validity of the practice is not confirmed, the innovator is likely to be discouraged from further experimentation, unless she/he has a high degree of self-confidence. There is also a high possibility that the results of the institutionalised scientist's methods could be invalid because of a non-holistic approach.

The indigenous knowledge system has been developed and is sustained differently from the Western scientific system. In the case of medicine, the theories are vastly different. Will verification based on the theories of Western science destroy traditional knowledge systems?

Against this, there appears to be a need for telling experimenters why their innovations work, since this could possibly help them use the theory to find quick solutions in other situations. It may be possible for institutional scientists to extract principles from the numerous practices, which could be further tested if necessary. A speeding up of the innovation processes is perhaps necessary now because of the possibility of climatic change altering environmental conditions rapidly.

Further, not all so-called traditional technologies are good, in their origins or in their results. Institutional scientists could help sift out the unsatisfactory ones, though the validity of their results would always be in doubt when one considers the need to take into account all the environmental as well as social effects of any technology.

Moreover, though Western scientific explanations could be found for traditional practices, most of the efforts to understand the "why" of what occurs are for the scientists' own intellectual pleasure.

Further, if such efforts are successful the innovations would probably be commercialised with possible harm to the innovators because, for instance, the availability, of plants whose products have been commercialised decreases.

What does it mean when farmers are told that institutional scientists appreciate their innovative work? Does it signify that it is important that such scientists check their research and verify it? Would this give the farmers the impression that the Western scientific system is "better" than theirs? The institutional scientists would then replace the peer group for farmer innovators.

The innovators are convinced that their technologies have succeeded. Such success may be only apparent. The farmers may have tried out various procedures earlier, one or more of which may have taken time to have an effect. It is probably normal practice for farmers to try out time-tested cures and only if they fail would they try innovations. The animal was on its way to being cured, anyway. There may have been some other reason for the cure: a plant grazed on by the animal which had curative properties, for instance. The farmers could have failed to understand that a cure following the use of a particular medicine does not always mean that the medicine has been the cause of the cure.

The farmer innovators "know" that their method works, institutional scientists question their knowledge. So what would be the effect of telling the innovators that their practices are useless? If the innovators' self-confidence is high enough to accept occasional failure, they would react by testing the suspect practices again; if they succeed, their self-confidence would be increased, if they fail it would be decreased but they may still be confident enough to carry on experimenting. If their self-confidence is low to start with, they would—in all probability—stop further innovations or stop communicating their knowledge lo others. They may not have the self-confidence to fail or to admit failure.

In many Indian laboratories, it is the lack of self-confidence to fail that limits the research undertaken to imitative research, to research for instance, which merely searches for new biochemicals or quantifies their occurrence in various parts of plants which have not been researched earlier. There is an obvious reluctance to attempt off-the-beaten-track research.

However, a question still remains: Can the traditional system of technology and the Westernised one survive concurrently? Every indication leads to the conclusion that institutional science tends to displace traditional technology wherever it reaches. This is not because it is superior in practice but because the educational, agricultural, economic and political sub-systems present traditional technology as old-fashioned, superstitious and useless, and

Western science and technology as modern, rational and capable of solving all problems. While there are always exceptions to this, the overall pressures to abandon traditional technology are very strong and not easily resistable.

If there is reliable evidence that the Western model of development cannot be promoted without destroying the traditional system, then it becomes necessary for institutionalised scientists to change. The traditional systems would need to be seen as the alternative models to the Western one.

III

Conclusion

Western society has absolute faith in the belief that a science and technology, designed to dominate Nature and other human beings, will be able to solve all of society's problems, including those of those who have been dominated.

Formal scientists have the responsibility of discovering whether this is true or not, even if it is unpalatable to them. Western science and technology appears to have inherent defects and limitations which have made a major contribution to the numerous social and environmental problems that exist. If at all Western science does find solutions to these problems, such solutions will most probably fast-breed still more—and worse—problems.

It has been claimed that Western science and its technology is neutral, but that it has been used by the Western industrial system in an unjust manner, and that those interested in justice can use that same science and technology for further justice. However, this is extremely unlikely given that its development requires huge quantities of funds, which can only be accumulated through an unjust system. If, for instance, all the people in a democracy agree to taxes which will pay for expensive research, it implies that those people have a high level of consumption which can only come from overuse of the earth's resources.

The direction in which the Western world is developing is not one which all of us must inevitably follow. We have choice between accepting the limited rationality of the Western system which makes it self-destructive and unjust, or fostering holistic knowledge systems and practices which are sustainable and more equitable. Common sense tells us that the survival of all is more important than scientifically reduced life on earth.

The urgent need, therefore, is to support and develop knowledge systems which do not have the limitations of Western science. Every effort should be made to replace it by liberation systems based on-but not necessarily identical with—traditional ones, since traditional technologies approach most closely the requirements of liberation technology. Such sciences can be the common heritage of all people, who can be, not merely passive recipients of the products of "experts", but creators of knowledge themselves. Research, which formal scientists have attempted to monopolise for the last few hundred years, can be returned to the masses.

There must be peoples' sciences—subsets of knowledge—since each region will have its own specific requirements, though they may be linked together at other levels. Such a system needs to be studied and practiced by everybody. Revitalising peoples' sciences can restore to millions the creativity and the power that has been appropriated from them. Their urgent preservation and restoration appears to be the only way to rebuild a sustainable society.

REFERENCES

1. Patriotic ft People-oriented Science & Technology Bulletin, inside front cover.
2. Kurt Mendelssohn, "Science And Western Domination", 1976, p 207.
3. ibid. p 77.
4. J A Conkling, "Pyrotechnics", Scientific American, July 1990, p 66.
5. Mendelssohn, op. cit. p 79.
6. ibid p 102.
7. ibid p 81.
8. ROS Herman, "Penetrating the Market", New Scientist, 30.9.89, p 68.
9. Ethical Dimensions, Alan Cottey, Chemistry & Industry, 16.3.92 219.
10. Frederick F Clairmonte, "Harvest Of The Holocaust", Economic & Political Weekly, 20.10.90, p 2365.
11. S. Lal, "Pathology Of Affluence", Times of India, 9.9.89.
12. Donald MacKenzie, "The Guiding Principles Of Nuclear War". New Scientist, 24.3.90 p 37.
13. David Noble, "Professors Of Terror: Scientists Who Maim And Kill", Third World Resurgence, February 1992 pp 34-35.
14. ibid.
15. Andrew Crowe, "Empty Promise", New Scientist, 13.1.90p 55.
16. See Susantha Goonatilake, "Crippled Minds", 1982.
17. Linda Gamlin, "Wallacism In Brief, New Scientist, 8.2.92 p 51.
18. See Stephen Jay Gould, "The Mismeasure of Man", 1981.
19. Rajesh Kochhar, Science As A Totem, Indian Express, 26.10.91.

20. Mendelssohn, op. cit. p 167
21. Colin Tudge, "Science for the Sake of It", New Scientist, 30.9.89, p 66.
22. R. K Kochhar, "Science As A Tool In British India", Economic & Political Weekly, 17.8.91 p 1927.
23. Kirkpatrick Sale, "The Conquest of Paradise, 1991, p 365.
24. Tony Travis, "Conventions And Cartels", Chemistry &t Industry 1.7.91 p 458.
25. Joseph Borkin, "The Crime and Punishment of 1. G. Farben, 1978, quoted in John Braithwaite, "Corporate Crime in the Pharmaceutical Industry", 1984, p 4.
26. Jonathan Glover, "Causing Death and Saving Lives", 1977, quoted in Braithwaite ibid.
27. Braithwaite ibid.
28. Little Change At The Top, Chemistry & Industry, 16.12.91 905.
29. Jurgen Habermas, "Knowledge ft Human Interests", p 4.
30. F Selleri, "Horns Of Venus", Science Today, June 1991 p 19.
31. David Hughes, "Rosencrantz and Guildenstern's Descendent", New Scientist, 13.7.91 p 49.
32. Priestlev, A Link Between British And American Chemical Societies, Chemical & Engineering News, 8. 4. 91 p 50.
33. Jim Baggott, "Davy, Faraday And The Royal Institution", New Scientist, 21.9.91 p 46.
34. Martha Crouch, "Confessions Of A Botanist", New Internationalist, March 1991 p 21.
35. "Physical Fears", New Scientist, 16.5.92 3.
36. "Physics Adds Muscle To British Industry", New Scientist, 16.5.92 10.
37. William Brown, "Britain Falls Behind In European Spending League", New Scientist, 6.10.90 p 18.
38. Elisabeth Geake, "Feed A Pensioner, Starve A Supercomputer", New Scientist, 14.12.91 p 14.
39. Simon Wolff, "How To Win Funds and Influence People", New Scientist, 1.2.91 p 57.
40. Stephen W Hawking, "A Brief History of Time", 1988 p 178.
41. Ed. Paul Davies, "The New Physics", 1989, reviewed and quoted in Scientific American, November 1989, p 105.

42. Stephanie Pain, "Sir Joseph's Buried Treasure", New Scientist, 17.3.90 p 57.
43. "Goodbye HIV?," New Scientist, 4.1.92 p 2.
44. Quoted in Jonathan Schell, "The Fate of the Earth", 1982, p 183
45. Hawking, op. cit. p 11.
46. ibid p 14.
47. Richard Elliot Benedick, "A Case Of Déjà vu", Scientific American, April 1992 p 120.
48. Hawking, op. cit. p 65.
49. ibid p 178.
50. ibid p 179.
51. ibid p 12.
52. Timothy O'Riordan, "A New Science for A New Age", New Scientist, 25.1.92 p 14.
53. Schell, op. cit. p 103.
54. Mendelssohn, op, cit. p 203.
55. L K Sharma, "Rediscovering Sin: Superb physics for a few bombs more". Times of India, 6.9.87.
56. Feedback, New Scientist, 4.5.91 p 54.
57. David Cohen, "War Games", New Scientist, 6.7.91 p 53.
58. M R Almeida, "Chitrak—A New Family Of Insectivorous Plants", Hornbill, October 1989 p 3.
59. Gary Stix, "Village Pharmacy", Scientific American, May 1992 p 87.
60. Jeffrey L Fox, US Biotechnology: Concern for The Future Of Bt Insecticides, Chemistry & Industry, 18. 11. 91 827.

About Earthcare Books :

We are a publisher and distributor focusing on environmental issues, justice and an alternative path of progress in harmony with nature and fellow humans.

The areas we emphasize are:

- Care of natural 'resources' (soil, water, forests, biodiversity...)
- Ecological (organic) farming and traditional systems
- Indigenous and other appropriate technologies
- Non-formal education and environmental education
- Natural health and healing
- Alternative lifestyles, cultures and world-views

EARTHCARE BOOKS
10 Middleton Street
Kolkata 700 071
INDIA
Phone : +91-33-22296551 / 22276190 / 022-2354242(
E-mail : earthcarebooks@gmail.com
Website : www.earthcarebooks.com

IPD
Bk 83638